Pen Pals

Marlene Pérez
Illustrated by Teresa Flavin

Rigby

Dear Miguel,

   My name is Elena. Our teacher asked if we would like to write to someone from another country. Isn't that a great idea?

   I asked for a pen pal from Mexico because my father was born there. He taught me a little Spanish, but I'll write to you in English.

   Please write to me!

                           Your pen pal,
                           Elena

P.S. I drew a map,
and I put a star to
show where I live.

Dear Elena,

It took a week for your letter to get to my school. Mrs. Rodriguez gave me the letter in class.

Thank you for the map. My little sister tried to draw on it!

Do you like to play sports? I play soccer a lot. I scored three times in my last game, and my team won.

Your pen pal,
Miguel

Dear Miguel,

    You really played great! I like to play soccer, and I'm on a team, too.

    Here is a picture of my soccer team.

    How old is your sister? I don't have any brothers or sisters, but I have a dog named Buster.

                 Your pen pal,
                 Elena

Dear Elena,

Thanks for the picture.

I don't have a dog, but I have a horse named Big Red.

My mom and dad own a bookstore. Sometimes I read to my sister while they help people find books. My sister is three years old. Here's a picture I drew of her.

What's it like where you live?

Your pen pal,
Miguel

Dear Miguel,

You draw very well. I wish I had a little sister.

Our apartment is near the beach. Here's a picture of Buster. He likes to chase sticks and splash in the water. What's it like where you live?

Your pen pal,
Elena

Dear Elena,

I live near the mountains. We have many horses. I like to ride my horse after school. Here we are together.

I would like to meet you! Would you like to come and visit us this summer? Have you ever been to Mexico?

Your pen pal,
Miguel

Big Red

Dear Miguel,

I would like to meet you, too! My dad said that we can drive to Mexico this summer.

I want to see where you live and meet your family. I want to meet Big Red, too!

Your pen pal,
Elena

Dear Mrs. Raymond,

   Hi! I'm visiting my
pen pal, Miguel, in Mexico.
We live in different places,
but we are alike in many
ways. Miguel drew a picture
of us.
   Thanks for helping me
find such a great friend!

   Your second grader,
   Elena

Mrs. Raymond
Kennedy Elementary School
1210 Front Street
Galveston, TX 77550